Between You & I…
28 Days with
Jesus

A Devotional Journey

Angelica Wilshire

Dear Deac. Elizabeth
Nothing's Impossible with
God! Sky is the limit for you.
God Bless you!
In Christ's love.
Angie
Wilshire

Between You & I…28 Days with Jesus, A Devotional Journey
Copyright © 2017 by Angelica Wilshire

ISBN : 978-1-54392-464-0

Song lyrics quoted are from the following Recording projects written by Angelica Wilshire: "Between You & I – A Collection of Love Letters" © 2012; and "Between You & I…Part 2" © 2017

Dedication

This book is dedicated first, to my Lord and Savior and first Love, Jesus Christ. Thank You Lord so much for placing priceless value on me. Thank You for leading me and so skillfully writing Your story on my heart even when I couldn't feel Your work. Your blood means more to me than anything. Thanks for being my Keeper. I pray that I will never stop growing, learning from and following – You.

Secondly, thank you to all the writers, particularly Christian writers that have come before me and have ministered to my life. You have powerfully wielded The Written WORD along with your own written words to help me see Jesus – The Word made flesh. Whether you have received public recognition/awards or not, God's work has flowed thru you to me and many others to make His will done. You are seen; You are precious; You have unlimited value in the Kingdom of God.

A special thanks to my Dad & Mom for your support, love for God & God's Word and each other (Happy 40th Anniversary!!). Thank you to my siblings, extended family, my church family FHC and the Body of Christ in Greater Boston / Massachusetts as well as all over the US and the World. May we shine bright for the King of kings.

Additional thanks to my mom, Naomi Wilshire, for review, editorial & ministerial comments, and encouragement on the writing of this book.

Last but never least, I want to dedicate this to any reader near or far that is looking to get closer to Jesus ; I have already prayed for you. Whether you are a long-time believer in Christ or have yet to believe, may this be the beginning of the best years of your life and all the generations that come after you. May the Lord's Kingdom come and perfect will be done here on earth in your life and everyone connected to you– as it is in Heaven, **In Jesus' name I pray – Amen.**

Table of Contents

PART 1:

PART 2:

Introduction

Dear Reader,

    I have written this devotional based on songs I have been inspired to write that have been a part of my prayer time and faith walk with Christ. Each day you will find a Scripture and a reflection based on the passage that leads you in prayer. Some of the prayers begin with words that I have prayed in my own life over the years. You will have space to write your own prayer or thoughts if you wish. Each day's devotional has a title that is named after a song I have written and recorded on one of my two recording projects. You don't need to have exposure to the particular song or buy any of the music to follow the devotional, however if you wish to compliment your time with listening to songs that relate to the day, you may learn about accessing the music at www.awilshiremusic.com .

    Lastly, if you are new to faith in Christ or perhaps haven't made a full step yet in believing in Jesus, but are going through this devotional as an initial step, I want to leave you with this scripture:

    "…anyone who wants to approach God must believe both that he exists *and* that he cares enough to respond to those who seek him." – Hebrews 11:6 (The Message)

    These next days, <u>choose</u> to enter this time believing that God hears you, is walking with you, and will answer you, even if you are at the beginning of your journey.

    May the Lord bless your walk with Him now and always.

Sincerely,

Angelica

Day 1 – Earnest Prayer

~

"Enter into His Gates with Thanksgiving..." (Psalms 100:4a - NKJV)

"Draw near to God and He will draw near to you" (James 4:8a - NKJV)

....

If you were to be completely honest with God at this moment and time of your life, what words would you use? What would your prayer look like? The song "Earnest Prayer" was the very first song I wrote during my mid-teen years and though the lyrics seem as though they are from a heart that could be super holy, super deep or mature, it really came from a heart that just wanted to draw close and be who God called. This heart was not yet reaching "the goal" but leaning forward for more. So if you are interested, I believe that spirit is a good place to start; with honesty and earnestness. As you spend more time with God, your desires and prayers will begin to bend to His will. However, you don't have to wait until then.

Before you start, take a minute to be quiet and search your heart about what has been going on with you. Next, share with Jesus in prayer 5 things you are thankful for. Even if it is a simple list, Scripture states that it is always best to begin with thanksgiving. Afterwards, be honest with Him, and believe that He hears you. You can't see Jesus but He is alive, here, ready to receive what He already knows is I your heart (so no need to fake it!)

"Dear Jesus, Thank You so much for drawing close right now. I want to come honestly before You and share what has been going on. Please hear me out and help me receive every bit of a response that You have for me. In your name I come and pray..."

11

I Want to be who God Called, and draw near to God (my Father). Spend time with God in pray, Your desires and pray will bend to Gods Will.

I Hankful for:
1) Being Saved and For Jesus my Savour & Lord
2) My Church Home and New Family in Christ
3) To Be able to see my childres grow and Grandkids
4) Answer to prayer
5) Gods Love - peace - Comfort - Help - provides Victory - Healing - Deliverence - Joy Supplying my needs - Continue Growth Gods Word

Day 2 – Dedication Song

~

"For God so loved the world that he gave his one and only Son, that whoever believes in him shall not perish but have eternal life." (John 3:16 - NIV)

....

One definition in the dictionary for the word "dedicate" is: "to devote wholly and earnestly, as to some person or purpose". (Dictionary.com)

It is weird to dedicate all of who you are to something or someone before you know everything about them or even that which you are committing to. The truth is that with God, though unchanging, we will be learning about Him for the rest of our lives and if that were not the case, He would not be God.

Even so, He remains so accessible. He actually made the first move towards us offering life itself before we even knew we had a choice to accept or deny it.

Life. Let us breathe that in and let that idea settle in. (Really...Go ahead – Breathe in deeply and then breathe out...)

A promise of Life here on earth and even after our days on earth has been offered. A promise of One who hears, knows and loves us every moment of the day and has the capability to do that perfectly - is for the taking.

I think the first step to dedication is believing in Christ. Once we do that, there is a journey of life that makes each one of our days a dedication song.

Dear God, thank You for sending Your Son – Jesus – so that I can have life. I believe in Him. Help my unbelief. I want the life You promised, not just after death, but here on earth. Thanks for dedicating Your life to me before I would even accept it. Teach me more. May this day be the start of my whole life being a true dedication song to You...

I dedicate (Devote) my life every day to the Lord. I will get to Know him every day as I go along and Walk with him. He gave His life so I Could have life. God offer His son Jesus in exchange for my life, so I Could have Eternal Life and the abundant life the Jesus Christ brings. And much more. God first loved me, before I ever loved him.

Day 3 – Alone With You

~

"...He (Jesus) said to them, "Come with me by yourselves to a quiet place and get some rest." - Mark 6:31b (NIV)

Being Alone.

It is not good for man to be alone.

I don't want to be alone.

Don't leave me alone.

All of the above statements stir up different thoughts and emotions in us; some valid; some nostalgic, as well as other things. A few of the statements may be something that you have said or thought specifically at one point in time. The truth is that we as people, need people; and balance is so important. We need friends. We need family. We need the Body of Christ regularly. All these are a gift from God. However, one thing we need in the midst of these is quality time in prayer with the Lord; One-on-one time. It may not be for a long time, but a time where our eyes are looking specifically on Him and our heart and mind is meditating on His Word. During this time, we share our true heart in honesty before Him. We are never alone. God is always there speaking through so many things throughout the day. God speaks through our friends, co-workers, situations, sermons, etc. Yet there is a space that can never replace one-on-one time with Jesus. He wants to hear **your** voice, **your** prayer, **your** confession, and **your** thanks. Your voice is not like any other person. You were made so uniquely. There is no other you and you are of great value to Him. He wants to give you rest, real rest. The more we get to know Jesus, the more we get to know who we are, love ourselves appropriately, and in turn, love our neighbors as we love ourselves.

So go ahead! Carve out some daily alone time with God. Take time to share your prayer request and desires. Take some time to really look at what He is saying in his Word and talk to Him about what you think He might have been showing you throughout the day. You may be led to talk to a friend, or get some counseling; let something go for good; ask for forgiveness; take the journey towards reconciliation with someone; or give love in some specific way out of this set-apart time. You may be entering a glorious season of intentionally receiving healing that Christ has wanted to pour into you for a long time, if you are willing. Yes, you can pray at any time, and yes, God speaks to hearts all throughout the day in many situations and settings, including in community in special ways. **But also,** the Lord speaks when you intentionally set some time aside and seek Him. It builds a relationship that no one can take away; and gets you away from the noise that can build up in the day. So go ahead, I dare you!

Dear Lord Jesus, I am here to spend time with You; I would like to do this daily. Show me the best place and method. Please speak to my heart ...

We hva people need people and one another. Gifts from God. We need the Lord and he wants us to come aside and spend time with him. God can speak to you in many different ways, and when you take time to be with him,

Day 4 – Right Here

~

"For to us a child is born, to us a son is given, and the government will be on his shoulders. And he will be called Wonderful Counselor, Mighty God, Everlasting Father, Prince of Peace." - Isaiah 9:6 (NIV)

"You make known to me the path of life; in your presence there is fullness of joy; at your right hand are pleasures forevermore." - Psalm 16:11 (ESV)

"God is our refuge and strength, an ever-present help in trouble." - Psalms 46:1 (NIV)

....

"Right Here Where there is peace in the midst of Storm. Where the love never fails and I am safe from Harm – Right here, this is where I belong Right here..." (Lyrics from song entitled "Right Here")

Right here. Right There. God is right there **with YOU**. You are never alone.

The above quoted lyrics is from a song I wrote during one of my college vacation breaks. I was in my room at home relaxing when this tune came to me. I do not think it was particularly a stormy season in life but I recall a sense of peace and rest as the tune came to my heart and I began to fumble with the words and then began to write them down.

The truth of the matter is that wherever God is, that is the place to be. As highlighted above, Scripture says that Jesus is to be called "Wonderful Counselor, Mighty God, Everlasting Father, and Prince of Peace". In a busy and crazy world, individually and collectively I would say we all need someone like this in our lives, and guiding our lives. Yes, He is everywhere but being close to Him, following His best for your life is the best gift you could give yourself this year. Therefore, I want to challenge you that this year you would come closer to Jesus.

Dear Jesus, thank You for being right here. Help me to commune with You today. I want You - Prince of Peace - guiding my life and I desire the fullness of joy that is promised in your presence - show me the path for my life...

God is with me, In good or bad times Know matter what, Right there !! Come closer to Jesus, he is everywhere you are. To Be your prince of peace, Mighty Counceler, Everlasting Father, Mighty God He is right there for you, Know matter what I am going through.

Day 5 – Worship Is

~

Therefore, I urge you, brothers and sisters, in view of God's mercy, to offer your bodies as a living sacrifice, holy and pleasing to God--this is your true and proper worship. - Romans 12:1 (NIV)

God is spirit, and his worshipers must worship in the Spirit and in truth." - John 4:24 (NIV)

....

Today - I will leave you simply with the words to a poem I wrote on Worship. These words came to me after years of walking with Christ (though still early in my life). They remain for me a reminder and coach of growing in worship, which is a daily and annual goal. Worship isn't just music. It is everything we can give, (spiritual, physical, emotional; hearts and minds, decisions, (everything!); bowing to all that the Triune-God is. May the above scriptures and below poem, lead you in prayer today.

Worship is TRUST
Trusting that God can change me, someone else or any circumstance in His time and in His own way
Trusting that He knows me better than I do
Trusting that the questions that I have will be answered
Trusting that every promise He has said will come to past

Worship is BEING REAL WITH GOD
Being real with God by letting him know what's bothering me at all times
Being real with God by accepting that I need His help in order to understand the past, present, and future

Worship is GIVING
Giving Him control of my thoughts, of my decisions,
of my habits and hopes, realizing that He is in control anyways
Giving my full attention to His word,

by which I allow Him to change my heart
Giving up my agenda in exchange for His agenda
Giving the Lord His due respect,
not offering up praises that originate solely from lips,
but rather, my heart
Giving the gifts which God has supplied to me, to others,
the greatest of these gifts being love

Worship is LISTENING
Listening for and to the voice of God
Listening to those who are in need of my attentive ear
Listening to discipline by which God shapes my heart

Worship is HUMBLING MYSELF
Not seeking recognition from men and women,
but honoring God with my heart

Worship is INTIMATE
A tight relationship with the Lord, of whom there is no one
or thing of greater importance in life

Dear Jesus, I want to be a worshipper; teach me how...

I persent my body, Holy and pleasing to God, Which is my True proper Worship to God.

Worship Is: Trusting - Be real with God - Giving God everything - Listening - Humbling - Intimate.

Trusting God in all things and everything and In behalf of others, Be honest and real with God, be your self and open, Telling God everything no matter what. Give God Control of everything, situations, habits, Thoughts etc,

Listen to Gods Voice and Know His Voice. Don't seek recognition from others. Honor God with your heart. Whole heart. Have an intamate relationship, close, real, honest, tight relation ship with God. There is no one or thing of greater importance in life. God is more important than any one or thing. Make Him first in your life and in all things.

Day 6 – Come To Me

~

"Come to me, all you that are weary and are carrying heavy burdens, and I will give you rest. Take my yoke upon you, and learn from me; for I am gentle and humble in heart, and you will find rest for your souls. For my yoke is easy, and my burden is light." - Matthew 11:28-30 (NRSV)

"Are you tired? Worn out? Burned out on religion? Come to me. Get away with me and you'll recover your life. I'll show you how to take a real rest. Walk with me and work with me—watch how I do it. Learn the unforced rhythms of grace. I won't lay anything heavy or ill-fitting on you. Keep company with me and you'll learn to live freely and lightly." - Matthew 11: 28-30 (The Message)

....

Wow! The above Scripture says it all. In reading it, two words stick out: 1) Come, and 2) Learn.

These two words are supported by colorful words/phrases such as "Weary"; "Carrying Heavy Burdens"; "Find Rest"; "Easy"; "Light". All these phrases in the above Scripture speak to the longing of the heart. It shows that Jesus knows exactly what's going on in our life and what we need. Our first step is to come to Jesus and in our coming, He asks us to learn from Him. Subsequently, He is going to do the relieving and helping us find rest.

I wrote a song called "Come to Me" in which I reflect on different situations that I and other people may have gone thru. Through it all Jesus was there. Jesus is here. He cares about your load. He understands the load and wants true rest for each of us. Let's come to Him and learn.

Dear Jesus here I am...

The Lord will give me rest, as I
Come to him and give him the burdens and
cares. Take the Lords yoke and learn his way
so I can live freely and lightly.
Come and learn.
Jesus knows what I need and what
is going on in my life. Jesus cares
Jesus is here for me, I can
Come to Jesus and find rest.

Day 7 – For Myself

~

"But whatever were gains to me I now consider loss for the sake of Christ. What is more, I consider everything a loss because of the surpassing worth of knowing Christ Jesus my Lord, for whose sake I have lost all things. I consider them garbage, that I may gain Christ and be found in him, not having a righteousness of my own that comes from the law, but that which is through faith in Christ—the righteousness that comes from God on the basis of faith. I want to know Christ—yes, to know the power of his resurrection and participation in his sufferings, becoming like him in his death, and so, somehow, attaining to the resurrection from the dead.

Not that I have already obtained all this, or have already arrived at my goal, but I press on to take hold of that for which Christ Jesus took hold of me. Brothers and sisters, I do not consider myself yet to have taken hold of it. But one thing I do: Forgetting what is behind and straining toward what is ahead, I press on toward the goal to win the prize for which God has called me heavenward in Christ Jesus." - Philippians 3:7-13 (NIV)

....

I grew up in a family where Christian ministry was / is a part of its fabric as much as would be getting dressed or eating your daily dinner. Growing up in such a setting made access to Scripture and testimonies of faith in Christ closer to me than perhaps others. Even so, in my journey in life, there came a point where I sensed the Lord beckoning me closer to know Him, not just through the faithfulness of my parents or grandparents; not solely through the songs we sang weekly in a community of faith; but for myself. I wrote a song about it realizing God's value on my life superseded all of that. Though I am so grateful for the rich heritage and the access to solid teaching and living that I've learned along the way, I know that it is what we do with the Word of God that matters most. It is about how we respond and live it. It is a choice that every person has to make whether they grew up around other Christians or are hearing about Jesus for the first time. I am so glad that Jesus came for all of us. **He died for me**. **He died for YOU**. I want to know this person that would put such value on my life. It is so awesome that He has revealed his truth to my parents and to the awesome teachers and Pastors in my midst. But it is even more incredible that He wishes to reveal Himself to me and through me. That is the type of value that He has placed on my life and yours. A love like that is worth getting to know intentionally. It will be a lasting journey that will inform, and keep fresh and whole any and all the ways God will call you to serve in His name. I want to know Jesus "For Myself". I invite you to join me.

Dear Jesus...

I Consider everything I had or have as lost. That I may know and became more Christ like. What God has for me and what Jesus Christ accomplish on the Cross for me, is far better than what I had or have. I release all to receive what God has for me. I forget what behind, after I deal with what I need to deal with. Then going ahead into my Destiny and what God has for me. What I do with Gods word matters most. I am to live it. and to walk the word of God out In my life. Father your way is the way I am to go. Your truth is the way I am to go. You are the way!!

Day 8 – This Love

~

"This is real love--not that we loved God, but that he loved us and sent his Son as a sacrifice to take away our sins." - 1 John 4:10 (NLT)

....

Love. In the United States we celebrate it on February 14th each year. For those who have given their life to Christ, there are a few other holidays that also helps us to celebrate love throughout the year.

December 25th: a celebration of God's love for the world by sending His one and only Son - Jesus.

Easter: a celebration of the weekend that Jesus willingly gave up His life for the world, died and rose on the third day giving access to all believers to the power of resurrection life. He didn't deserve to die but He took the blame to cover our sin.

Even **Thanksgiving** in November of each year: the day that we give thanks for all the gifts of love that we receive in every way.

Love is all around us. I write this chapter on Valentine's Day (how ironic!) Many view love as purely romantic. The Bible speaks of love in many ways: between a Bridegroom and His Bride; Between The Father and His Children; The love of a good friend; even loving your enemy, and much more! The Bible says: "God is Love". So much guidance on love, we can study it for the rest of our lives. I wrote a song called "This Love" and a part of the lyrics state:

"It was Your love that reached out and touched me; To constantly give - not an ordinary thing; With open arms, devotion pursued me; My heart is overwhelmed - No more pain now I can feel - This Love."

In this song, I reflect on what God's love means to me overall and also specifically when I remembered a time of experiencing such disappointment that the heartache was physical in nature. For months I walked around with a pain that felt real. But as I persisted in prayer and staying close to the Lord, with the help of Godly friends and the Lord Himself, I woke up one day - and the pain was gone. This song was partially birthed through that specific memory. Even so, God's love is so much more than a feeling. His love was there for me even when I couldn't feel it; so I know that depending on feelings alone is a lost cause. God's love is available to you too, whether you are in a season that seems mundane, uneventful, perfect, or if your life feels very tumultuous. I pray that you experience "This Love" now and forever, unceasingly. Today I pray this prayer from Scripture over you: Specifically,

"that Christ may dwell in your hearts through your faith. And may you, having been [deeply] rooted and [securely] grounded in love, be fully capable of comprehending with all the saints (God's people) the width and length and height and depth of His love [fully experiencing that amazing, endless love]; and [that you may come] to know [practically, through personal experience] the love of Christ which far surpasses [mere] knowledge [without experience], that you may be filled up [throughout your being] to all the fullness of God [so that you may have the richest experience of God's presence in your lives, completely filled and flooded with God Himself]". - Ephesians 3:17-19 (AMP)

God Love me enough to send His son
Jesus Christ to take away my sins.
God is love, love comes from God.
God will always love me. God
my Heavenly Father wants me to
Know and experience His love.
And to walk in and show His
love. Gods love works and is
In me. I am to express Gods

love in me. I can love and show love. Gods love, not the worlds idea of ~~love~~ love. Gods love is <u>unconditional</u>.

Day 9 – More

~

"Now to Him who is able to do exceedingly abundantly above all that we ask or think, according to the power that works in us, to Him *be* glory in the church by Christ Jesus to all generations, forever and ever. Amen." - Ephesians 3:20-21 (NKJV)

....

The above passage is so powerful.

It is so awesome to even let your mind go to the place that God is able to do abundantly above all that we ask or think. We human beings know how to dream. God has given us an amazing imagination and it is as if He *wants* us to dream. The cool thing is, He wants us to dream **with** Him and He wants do the works **in** us. What a wonderful relational God.

My immediate prayer response to the above Scripture is: *"Lord, Help me believe You and help me to come to You with dreams that are bigger than my current capacity. Give me wisdom and courage, and help me not minimize You to human strength."*

Can I tell you a secret? I created a "Dream" page on this online scrapbook program called "Pinterest" (which is so fun to use!!). I made this Dream page saving pictures of things I want to see and have in my life. I made the page private and I have been praying through my dreams intently, asking God for the gift of these dreams and also wisdom and His opinion about them.

I challenge you today to do the same. Maybe you aren't into Pinterest, but I know that you have a pen and paper. Start writing down your dreams and entrust them to Jesus. There is a passage of Scripture in **1 Thessalonians 5:23 (NIV)** that says:

"May God himself, the God of peace, sanctify you through and through. May your whole spirit, soul and body be kept blameless at the coming of our Lord Jesus Christ. The one who calls you is faithful, and he will do it."

This prayer in and of itself would take only an all-powerful God to accomplish – to make your WHOLE spirit, soul and body be kept blameless. However the next verse says, *"The one who calls you is faithful, and he will do it".* If the Apostle Paul, who wrote the prayer, can believe God with confidence for something that no human being has the capacity to do, how much more can we offer up our other dreams with great expectation? Let's do that now.

Dear Lord Jesus, Thank You so much for Your abundant power. Please work in me greater than all I could ever imagine. I offer these dreams and desires to you today...

God is able to do all. That we could ever ask or thing. Everything. God is greater then human strength. God is faithfull. What he says He will do. Do what?? Keep my Body-Soul and spirit Blamess before the Lords coming. faithfull to keep His word/promises. God is able to do everything. put Your Trust on God Your father for everything and the impossibles. According to the power that works in us. (faith/power).

Day 10 – I Will Remember You

~

"...in everything give thanks; for this is the will of God in Christ Jesus for you." - 1 Thessalonians 5:18 (NKJV)

"The Son (Jesus Christ) is the radiance of God's glory and the exact representation of his being, sustaining all things by his powerful word. After he had provided purification for sins, he sat down at the right hand of the Majesty in heaven." - Hebrews 1:3 (NIV)

"Look to him, and be radiant; so your faces shall never be ashamed." - Psalms 34:5 (NRSV)

....

Counting your blessings is not a new concept. It is sung in many songs, spoken by many leaders (Christian and secular) and also Scripture speaks clearly about how important it is to give thanks. If we aren't clear on God's will for our life, we can start there.

Remembering God and His work in my life and throughout time is something that has been so important.

We can get so bogged down with the troubles of life; the next need; the opinions of others; even the flashing and exciting things, that we can miss out on seeing what's true and best. Looking to God is a direct tie to the degree of radiance and light that emanates from our life. Also, it is a great guard against shame. Looking to God includes noticing all the ways He is blessing, but also includes learning about Him and recounting His nature. It can also include relying on, and taking refuge in, Him. So if you don't know where to begin in looking at or remembering God, here are a few places to begin (or restart!):

1. **Give thanks.** Decide to write down and even speak out 10 blessings/gifts that you noticed from your day, for the next 31 days this month. You'll begin to let God into

perspective just by noticing the gifts He gives. If you have been walking with Christ for any period of time, think weekly of some times in the past that stood out as key moments where God answered you specifically or moved in your life.

2. **Get to know Jesus even more** by reading about His life. All of Scripture speaks of and points to Christ, but starting with the gospels (Matthew, Mark, Luke and John) is a great place as you can read about His life and read His words as recorded by those who walked with Him.

3. For the different Holidays this year, think of ways you can **celebrate** in **God** by remembering Him in those celebrations.

4. **Pray about all of your concerns**. Let The Lord know and ask for guidance. This too is remembering God.

5. If you don't already, prayerfully **consider** making a priority **gathering regularly with** others who prioritize following and loving Christ and God's written Word (The Bible), via **a great local church.**

Dear Jesus, may today be a commitment/recommitment of me remembering You consistently for the rest of my days...

Looking at all the ways God is blessing me. Help me Lord to see all the ways you are blessing me. And to see were your hands are upon my life. Help me Lord to give you Thanks in all things. Learn to know God and His nature. pray about everything, let the Lord guard you. Gather = other people of God who follow and love Christ and Gods word. Remember the Lord at all times.

Day 11 – You Are Mine

~

'But now, this is what the Lord says— he who created you, Jacob, he who formed you, Israel: "Do not fear, for I have redeemed you; I have summoned you by name; you are mine...Since you are precious and honored in my sight, and because I love you...'" - Is 43:1&4a (NIV)

"Know that the Lord is God. It is he who made us, and we are his; we are his people, the sheep of his pasture." - Ps 100:3 (NIV)

"For you created my inmost being;   you knit me together in my mother's womb. I praise you because I am fearfully and wonderfully made; your works are wonderful..." - Psalms 139:13-14 NIV)

"No one has ever seen God, but the one and only Son, who is himself God and is in closest relationship with the Father, has made him known." - John 1:8 (NIV)

"For God so loved the world that He gave His only begotten Son, that whoever believes in Him should not perish but have everlasting life.." - John 3:16 (NKJV)

....

God speaks words of love to human beings all throughout history; through scripture, through His works and most importantly through His son, Jesus Christ, Lord of all. Jesus is the greatest love letter that we will ever experience in life. The more we get to know Him the more we will understand how precious we are and who we are.

I am trying to let you know that you are of great value to God. Jesus' life itself is proof of that. You are precious to Him - all of you: your personality; your body; your heart; your soul; your heritage. He literally died for it all.

Take a read to lyrics to the song "You Are Mine" that I wrote on the next page. These lyrics were birthed right in the midst of one of the hardest seasons of my life. There were people passing away right and left. I felt far away from my loved ones and just overwhelmed by things happening around me. Processing it all just didn't seem to be happening fast enough. In the midst of the chaos, death, disappointment, loneliness, even some of the exciting times that were happening simultaneously, this song came to my heart. It is so interesting to realize that in the midst of chaos there is possibility to access stillness and truth - by the grace of God. I believe this song was one of God's gifts to me. It was solely His rescue; His keeping me grounded and aware of His nearness, love and desire for me, in the midst of everything.

Jesus loves us, in the midst of _____ (fill in the blank with something related to your life). Now repeat that sentence again to yourself.

Wherever you are, you were His idea. You are His creation and He wants your heart so you can agree with His Word and truly say, "I am Yours".

You Are Mine - By Angelica Wilshire

Beauty can't describe, what I had in mind,

the moment you first were conceived

One of a kind; at your completion I smiled;

fashioned within so perfectly

Fearfully and wonderfully made;

a perfect gift that I'd never trade

Precious in my sight; reflector of my light;

you are the one that I choose

I love to hear your voice; by far you are my choice;

will spend eternity showing you

That my love pursues to the end;

I'll be your comforter and a good friend

You are mine,

and each moment I wait for your heart to turn to Mine

You are mine,

you look all about but I am right there by your side

I wish you'd stop and see; spend some time with Me

You are mine and I love just what I made;

You are mine and I love just what I made

Dear Lord, I am yours...

I am not to fear. The Lord has redeemed me, summons me (called me) by name. I belong to the Lord, I am his. The Lord loves me, I am precious and honoured in his sight. God created me, knitted me when I was in my mothers womb. I Belong to God. Jesus loves me in the midst of: what ever um going through my actions, Reactions no matter what. He wants my heart, so I can agree with His word. and say, "I am yours". God wont trade me. I am one of a Kind.

Day 12 –
This is My Calling (Song of the Beloved)

~

"...I urge you to live a life worthy of the calling you have received. Be completely humble and gentle; be patient, bearing with one another in love. Make every effort to keep the unity of the Spirit through the bond of peace. There is one body and one Spirit, just as you were called to one hope when you were called; one Lord, one faith, one baptism; one God and Father of all, who is over all and through all and in all." - Ephesians 4:1-6 (NIV)

....

Just as a bridegroom and bride become one in marriage, those who have given their life to Christ are one with Him and are a part of the Body of Christ. This body, though many and different in gifts and such, they are One. This Body is even denoted collectively in Scripture as the Bride of Christ. When you give your life to Jesus, you are not just one of God's creations, you become His Beloved One. It is a beautiful and unique calling, that you grow in as the days and years go by and as you learn to follow Christ. Let's not settle with just any old calling, let's go for the calling that is worthy, that sometimes isn't easy but is oh so glorious because of connection to the One who is calling. Step into your identity as The Lord's Beloved One - I dare you!

Dear Jesus, help me to live a life worthy of the calling You have for my life. Show me where to start and/or where to step next...

I am one with Christ and with my Brothers and Sisters. I am to walk worthy of my Calling. In love, gentleness, Kindness, peace, humble, patience. I am in the Body of Christ

My Calling is unique, I am to walk in my Calling. I am In the Body of Christ. My Calling is unique. I am the Lords Beloved one.

Day 13 – In My Presence

~

"Jerusalem will be told: "Don't be afraid. Dear Zion, don't despair. Your God is present among you, a strong Warrior there to save you. Happy to have you back, he'll calm you with his love and delight you with his songs." - Zephaniah 3:17 (The Message)

....

There is so much to learn in the different books of Scripture that a mere pass-over of one verse in the midst of a chapter could do harm in one's learning and understanding what God was doing at the time, and also is doing now in the hearts of readers. However, in the above passage one encouraging thing that is worth looking at (among many), is - **God sings**. God creates songs and even more, He uses them to calm people with His love. I want you today to not only understand that God is powerful, not only is He fierce and able to save, He also is present to us, caring, calming and shows all of that through His very own songs. In the New Testament of Scripture Jesus was referred to as "Immanuel" which means "God with us". God is present and can create new songs, even a new song playlist or soundtrack to the theme of your life just by being present; that is how powerful He is. This week, I encourage you to find 10 God songs that encourage and calm you and, in prayer, invite Christ Jesus to speak to you during your time of listening to the songs. Keep a notepad of what you notice throughout the week that is encouraging, comforting, calming and any "AHA" moments you might have throughout the week. Who knows, maybe an original song may result that is Between You & Him. It could just be your answer to prayer.

Dear Jesus, I invite Your songs into my life now, this week and forever. Have Your way in Your name I pray...

Don't be afraid, God is with me,
A strong Warrior, to save me.

God sings. A song can be just the answer to your prayer's. God can speak to you through a Song, scriptures, person, child, Bill Board and in many ways.

Day 14 – Walkin' Worthy

~

"And I saw a mighty angel proclaiming in a loud voice, "Who is worthy to break the seals and open the scroll?" But no one in heaven or on earth or under the earth could open the scroll or even look inside it. I wept and wept because no one was found who was worthy to open the scroll or look inside. Then one of the elders said to me, "Do not weep! See, the Lion of the tribe of Judah, the Root of David, has triumphed. He is able to open the scroll and its seven seals." Then I saw a Lamb, looking as if it had been slain, standing at the center of the throne, encircled by the four living creatures and the elders. The Lamb had seven horns and seven eyes, which are the seven spirits of God sent out into all the earth. He went and took the scroll from the right hand of him who sat on the throne. And when he had taken it, the four living creatures and the twenty-four elders fell down before the Lamb. Each one had a harp and they were holding golden bowls full of incense, which are the prayers of God's people. And they sang a new song, saying: "You are worthy to take the scroll and to open its seals, because you were slain, and with your blood you purchased for God persons from every tribe and language and people and nation. You have made them to be a kingdom and priests to serve our God, and they will reign on the earth." - Revelation 5:2-10 (NIV)

"With this in view we constantly pray for you, that our God may deem *and* count you worthy of [your] calling and [His] every gracious purpose of goodness, and with power may complete in [your] every particular work of faith (faith which is that leaning of the whole human personality on God in absolute trust and confidence " - 1 Thessalonians 1:11 (AMP)

....

What a powerful heavenly scene in the last book of the Bible. We read of Jesus, the Lamb, the only one who is worthy enough to open up this sealed scroll referenced. In all of heaven and earth, only one was worthy. But wait, there's more: This sole worthy One decides to purchase with His very own blood every person from every tribe and every nation - to make each person, Man and Woman together, a Kingdom and Priests. These people, who were not worthy, He purchased for them to be His, to Serve God and to reign on the earth. Do you know who these people are? They are you and I; Our families and our neighbors. But those who get to walk in this glorious calling are those who put their faith in Christ, confessing their sins, repenting and turning to Him. The second passage shows that after we come to Christ we are urged to live a life worthy of our calling. Jesus has called you. You are special. According to Psalms 139:14, you are "fearfully and wonderfully made", a marvelous work of God. You are worthy. Why? Because the One who is Worthy made you so and called you to be so.

Dear Jesus, Thank You for being You - and for purchasing me with Your very own blood. I want to walk worthy, show me how.

Jesus died and shed his blood for every person on earth. To make us Kingdom and priests. Live your life Worthy of your Calling, You are special. Fearfully and Wonderfully made. I am Gods marvelous work, I am Worthy, because of the who is worthy Made me. Help me to Walk Worthy Lord, show me how.

Day 15 – So Amazing

~

"Now to him who is able to do immeasurably more than all we ask or imagine, according to his power that is at work within us, [21] to him be glory in the church and in Christ Jesus throughout all generations, for ever and ever! Amen." - Ephesians 3:20 (NIV)

"Now to the God who can do so many *awe-inspiring things, immeasurable things,* things greater than we ever could ask or imagine through the power at work in us, [21] to Him be all glory in the church and in Jesus the Anointed from this generation to the next, forever and ever. Amen." - Ephesians 3:20 (The Voice)

....

Have you ever been amazed by something or someone? It is a feeling that is so wonderful and includes wonder, surprise, delight and exceeded expectations. I don't know about you but that is an experience that I wouldn't mind a little bit more of in my life.

The above Scripture makes the claim that God is able to exceed anything we could ever ask or even imagine. Wow, that is amazing. Whether we have been walking with Christ for a day or for over 25 years, God's character and ability remains the same. My prayer is that God will show you all the amazing things He has in store for you and that He is doing even now. May not even one thing go unnoticed by the eyes of your heart.

Dear Jesus, I invite you to amaze me. Work in every part of my life and let me testify that You are so amazing, in specific ways, in my life in every season.

God Can do everything and all things. Nothing Impossible with God. Exceedenly, abuntaly all and every thing. God is amazing, awsome, Wonderful.

49

Day 16 – Never A Time

~

"Where can I go from your Spirit? Where can I flee from your presence? If I go up to the heavens, you are there; if I make my bed in the depths, you are there. If I rise on the wings of the dawn, if I settle on the far side of the sea, even there your hand will guide me, your right hand will hold me fast. If I say, "Surely the darkness will hide me and the light become night around me," even the darkness will not be dark to you; the night will shine like the day, for darkness is as light to you." - Psalms 139:7-12 (NIV)

....

The Truth is that even if we stray from God and have no right to be in His perfect awesome presence, He knows where we are. He sees us and understands perfectly. He has 20/20 vision on every detail related to each of us. There is no dark place, no hell-ish place that can keep us from Him.

Even with this powerful truth, we do have to draw near, and there is a process to experience the fullness that Jesus died for us to have. There may be some surrendering or some things that we need to lay aside and get rid of. However, Jesus' eyesight is never dim and you are never out of sight. You are never so far away that He can't detect your cry or your whereabouts (for good or bad). I wrote a song called "Never a Time". It reminds me that in the ups and downs of my life; times where I felt great, times when I felt lost or even actually was a bit lost; times when people who I thought treasured me did not act in ways that were loving or treasuring; times when I literally felt like love was lost when it came to my life: Jesus was always there. He didn't leave me. He wasn't missing. Love was still there. I couldn't always feel it, but He was there. Here are some of the lyrics:

> "There's never a time that You're not with me;
> Never a time that You're not near me;
> Never a time; Never a time; Never a time

There's never a time that you're not faithful;
Never a time that You're not able;
Never a time that Love disappears;
Never a time...Nothing's Impossible with You...."

We are dealing with an unlimited God who even took initiative to address the impossible: sinful people being near a perfect God and thus experiencing forgiveness and change. He did this through Jesus. Even if you are dealing with missing the mark by a long shot, Scripture says: **"My dear children, I write this to you so that you will not sin. But if anybody does sin, we have an advocate with the Father—Jesus Christ, the Righteous One. He is the atoning sacrifice for our sins, and not only for ours but also for the sins of the whole world."** (1 John 2:1 – NIV). There is hope for every person: This gift is expensive. This gift is lasting.

Dear Jesus, I know now You are always with me; You always have been. Help me walk closely with You from this moment on...

There is no hedding from God. God sees You. Day and night are the same to God. Nothing can keep us from Him. I am never out of Jesus sight. He has more than 20/20 Vision. Jesus is there and with me and loves me, even when others don't show love. Depend on the Lords Love, Gods love. For Gods love and His ways are not like people (Humans) Depend and seek His love. He will

52

Never leave you, forshake you, abanding you, reject you, betroy you, lie to you. My God is with me and for me

Day 17 – Magnificat (Luke 1:46-55)

~

"My soul glorifies the Lord and my spirit rejoices in God my Savior, for he has been mindful of the humble state of his servant. From now on all generations will call me blessed, for the Mighty One has done great things for me— holy is his name. His mercy extends to those who fear him, from generation to generation. He has performed mighty deeds with his arm; he has scattered those who are proud in their inmost thoughts. He has brought down rulers from their thrones but has lifted up the humble. He has filled the hungry with good things but has sent the rich away empty. He has helped his servant Israel, remembering to be merciful to Abraham and his descendants forever, just as he promised our ancestors." - Luke 1:46-55 (NIV)

"Understand, then, that those who have faith are children of Abraham." - Galatians 3:7 (NIV)

....

The above first passage is an excerpt from Scripture and is actually a song written by Mary, the mother of Jesus. Mary wrote this song when visiting her cousin, Elizabeth, who was pregnant around the same time she was pregnant. When they met, it is recorded that the baby inside Elizabeth leaped. After words of blessing and power were pronounced over Mary by her cousin, Mary recited the above song recording what God had done for her by choosing, helping and blessing her.

I found the words of Mary's song, words that have now become my own life song as I have walked through the ups and downs of life with Christ. As a result, I put my own personal medley to these special words. God's will is that all people would experience these blessings. Through faith in Christ, this is possible.

My prayer for you is that these words will become your own testimony sooner than later; That you will be able to speak greatly of the Lord just as Mary has because of the personal experience of relationship you will enjoy with Christ. My prayer is that you will be able to say the following: "From now on all generations will call me blessed, for the Mighty One has done great things for me - Holy is His name"...

Dear Jesus, please make the words of Mary's song my very own testimony. Strengthen and grow my faith...

All nations and people will call me Blessed. Because of what they will see what the Lord has done in me and for me. And all the Great things! Holy is His name.

My Soul and spirit the rejoice and glorify the Lord God my Savior. Holy is His name for ever. He has performed mighty deeds, he has helped is servant and remembers His servant His promises are sure — True and forever amen!! I Love you Lord!!

Day 18 – Best

~

"This is what the Lord says— your Redeemer, the Holy One of Israel: "I am the Lord your God, who teaches you what is best for you, who directs you in the way you should go." Isaiah 48:17 (NIV)

"Do you not know that in a race all the runners run [their very best to win], but only one receives the prize? Run [your race] in such a way that you may seize the prize *and* make it yours!" - 1 Corinthians 9:24 (AMP)

"Whatever you do [whatever your task may be], work from the soul [that is, put in your very best effort], as [something done] for the Lord and not for me..." - Colossians 3:23 (AMP)

'You say, "I am allowed to do anything"--but not everything is good for you. You say, "I am allowed to do anything"--but not everything is beneficial.' – 1 Corinthians 10:23 (NLT):

....

What would it look like for you to give God your very best in this season? Different seasons call for different responses. The truth is He knows what truly is best for us, and yet we have wisdom today to offer ourselves in the best way possible to the One who is the only one who deserves it. My best may look a bit different from yours. Take this time to meditate on the above Scriptures and then schedule some intentional time this week to seek God about your life. You could go to a cafe or enjoy a nice dinner. Bring your Bible and a notepad; or you can spend some quiet time in another favorite spot. I enjoy places in the city by the water, but you may enjoy a comfortable corner in your home/room. There are good actions and then there is what is the "Best". Do not relent until you have clarity on what is best. Until you have clarity, persist in what you already know is best, until you understand more. In each season, it would be a great habit to go through this exercise, and as you seek the Lord, He will give you clarity and answers.

Dear Jesus, what would "The Best" look like in my life this season? How can I give you my best? There are so many different parts of my life, give me discernment. Like David said in Psalms 139:23 & 24 (NIV), "Search me, God, and know my heart; test me and know my anxious thoughts. See if there is any offensive way in me, and lead me in the way everlasting."

The Lord Teaches me what is best for me, Directs me in the way I should go. Run the race to the finish. You can do anything you want, but not anything you want to do is prophetable. God knows what is best for me. Seek the Lord and he will give your Clarity and answers

Day 19 – Rest in Me

~

"Come to me, all you who are weary and burdened, and I will give you rest". - Matthew 11:28 (NIV)

....

I don't know about you but a promise of rest is one of the best promises ever. Rest could be needed because of any of the following reasons:

- Life bringing you weeks of nonstop busy-work;
- Times of unexpected sickness, mourning, or hardship;
- The hype and the joy of completing a project that you enjoy and love;

Life changing rest can come after taking an obedient step towards God, giving your life to Christ for the first time or doing something you know He wants you to do.

Everyone needs rest. Rest is a gift from God. Also, true rest is something that God speaks of in Scripture in both the Old Testament and the New Testament. It is a promise for every season. The above passages contain the words of Jesus Himself. If ever you want rest, coming to Jesus is the best place to begin. I wrote a song called "Rest in Me" after finishing my first cd project. It took a lot of effort and I didn't realize it was like a birthing process until I was done. I was exhausted. I was so tired even though the work was so much fun. I remember finding a spot in area hotel that had a beautiful large window looking out to harbor waters. With my journal in hand, I prayed to the Lord and the following words came to mind:

> *"Rest in Me, there's no more need to fear; I am here*
> *Rest in Me. You've given, you've run, you've been faithful.*
> *Rest in Me. What you're lacking, I will be,*
> *From this Moment on, your heart will be my home.*
> *Rest in Me; the old has gone; the New is now come,*
> *Rest in Me. My Strength will be Your Strength*
> *Rest in Me - You're greatest fear; I have overcome*

and because you're Mine you too have overcome..."
(Lyrics from the song "Rest in Me").

I went on from the quiet time to finish this song about rest. I know that without turning to the Lord, my ability to bounce back and receive true rest would not have happened. What are you in need of right now? Take this time to pray and ask The Lord to give you the rest you need and show you what related steps would be helpful.

Dear Jesus, I want the rest that you have for me; I come to you now....

Take your rest in God, Receive and accept His Rest, in every situation that you go through. Rest Comes from God. Gods promise for every season. To give us Rest. Give me rest Lord Jesus. Help me to Come to you, to recieve Rest that only Comes from you.

Day 20 – You Are

~

'When Jesus came to the region of Caesarea Philippi, he asked his disciples, "Who do people say the Son of Man is?" They replied, "Some say John the Baptist; others say Elijah; and still others, Jeremiah or one of the prophets." "But what about you?" he asked. "Who do you say I am?" Simon Peter answered, "You are the Messiah, the Son of the living God." Jesus replied, "Blessed are you, Simon son of Jonah, for this was not revealed to you by flesh and blood, but by my Father in heaven.' - Matthew 16:13-17 (NIV)

....

In the above passage, Jesus checks in with His followers; the people who have been walking with Him and following Him for some time. He wants to find out what they hear from others about who He is. That question is a precursor to the real question: Who is it that they say He is? - The ones who have been walking Him; listening to His words? Today is Day 20 and you may be new to spending quality time with the Lord, or this may be another avenue to get closer. Either way, this a great time for a heart check. What about you? Who do YOU say Jesus is? Take this time to lift up a prayer of confession by answering this question and confessing aloud in prayer who He is to you. Be honest. God honors honesty more than flowery words. Also, take this time to invite Jesus to be even more. Invite Him to become all that He wants to be in your life.

Dear Jesus...

The Father reveals who Jesus is. Jesus is my healer, deliver, peace, joy, calm, Relaxer, Happyness, provider, Battle fighter, Hiding place, restorer, Intersessor, Victor, Conquer, Lord, Savior, High priest, mediator, Begining, ending, Eternal Life,

Truth, the way, light.

Day 21 – Worthy Is the Lamb

~

"The Lamb came and took the scroll from the right hand of the One seated upon the throne. And when He took it, the four living creatures and twenty-four elders fell prostrate before the Lamb. They worshiped Him, and each one held a harp and golden bowls filled with incense (the prayers of God's holy people). Then they sang a new song. Four Living Creatures and 24 Elders: You are worthy to receive the scroll, to break its seals, Because You were slain. With Your blood, You redeemed for God people from every tribe and language, people from every race and nation. You have made them a kingdom; You have appointed them priests to serve our God, and they will rule upon the earth. When I looked again, I heard the voices of heavenly messengers (numbering myriads of myriads and thousands of thousands). They surrounded the throne, the living creatures, and the elders. Thousands of Messengers *(with a great voice)*: Worthy is the Lamb who was slain. *Worthy is the Lamb* to receive authority and wealth and wisdom and greatness And honor and glory and praise." - Revelations 5:7-12 (The VOICE)

....

Once again, in this beautiful throne room scene we see Jesus, "The Lamb", being the only one in all of heaven and earth who has the capability of opening up this sealed scroll. The watchers, some with rank, realize in this action who is before them and their response is to fall down / bow down and worship and sing a new song declaring the Lamb's worth. They realize that the slain Lamb they were dealing with is the King of kings.

There are times after writing a song where I have this recurring "aha" moment. I realize of all of the wonderful and worthwhile songs and lyrics that exist, there really is only One that deserves the highest form of adoration and words of love consistently. I love a good love song, let me tell you! I am a romantic at heart. Human love songs have their place. However, even the best love song does not compare to the words that are due to the One who put a forever love on the line in advance for those who may or may not believe in Him or want Him. I realize that professing God's worth is the best experience one can participate in. Why? Because He is the only one who really deserves flawless and unending worship. I realize that I am participating in a pure and true act. Jesus is flawless yet took on all our flaws out of great love, to redeem us. You know that rush when you experience a good song? Well Jesus is the only one who <u>always</u> deserves the highest point of that love; His character can hold the weight of that rush at every moment. He is so deep, so consistent, He doesn't get old. There is so much to learn about Him. Jesus is worthy and has made you and I worthy by His own blood for those who receive Him. **Worthy is the Lamb.**

Lord Jesus, thank You for who You are and what You have done for me. I want to know You better in every season. As I walk through life let me always see You and seek You – Worthy One – and worship you appropriately – with my words, with my body, with my heart, and with my life, Teach me how. Thank You for redeeming me. Please help me to live the life You have purposed for me...

Jesus is the Lamb of God who is worthy to be Worshiped and praise. The Blood of Jesus save, brings all nations, people to be priest unto God, and walk as kings & priest and to serve God. Jesus has made me (us) worthy by His Blood. Worthy is the Lamb. Jesus deserves endless praise and Worship.

Day 22 – If

~

"What, then, shall we say in response to these things? If God is for us, who can be against us? He who did not spare his own Son, but gave him up for us all—how will he not also, along with him, graciously give us all things?" - Romans 8:31-32 (NIV)

....

God is for you.

God **IS** for you.

God is **FOR** you.

God is for **YOU**.

What good news is this! How awesome! The One that is over everyone, even the most powerful being and systems; the One whose sole opinion matters the most ; the One who has the power to open and close immovable doors ; The One who thought of and created every living thing in all their intricate and beautiful splendor... is for you. Therefore the question is, if this is true then.... (Fill in the blank). If this is true, what does this good news mean for your life? If this this is real - What lies or struggles would such a newsflash change for you? If this is possible, what areas of your life could this impact? What could you or would you do differently if you really believed this? If...If...If...

Take some time to pray and then to write down and list out all that comes to mind.

Dear Jesus, The Bible tells me that God is for me, how can I live my life differently in light of this truth? Help me really understand and run with this promise...

God is for me, Nothing Nor Anything can be against me,

God is Greater then anything That I will ever go through, Greater then the Devil - Demons - Trials - Betrayel Sickness - anixety - fear - worry - Loneliness - proverty - fear - threats - people - authority figures - Anything and all things.

Day 23 – To Notice You

~

"Blessed are the pure in heart, for they will see God." - Matthew 5:8 (NIV)

"No one has ever seen God, but the one and only Son, who is himself God and is in closest relationship with the Father, has made him known." - John 1:18 (NIV)

"However, as it is written: "What no eye has seen, what no ear has heard, and what no human mind has conceived"— the things God has prepared for those who love him" - 1 Corinthians 2:9

"The eye is the lamp of your body. When your eye is clear [spiritually perceptive, focused on God], your whole body also is full of light [benefiting from God's precepts]. But when it is bad [spiritually blind], your body also is full of darkness [devoid of God's word]." - Luke 11:34 (AMP)

"Therefore, since we are surrounded by so great a cloud of witnesses [who by faith have testified to the truth of God's absolute faithfulness], stripping off every unnecessary weight and the sin which so easily *and* cleverly entangles us, let us run with endurance *and* active persistence the race that is set before us, [looking away from all that will distract us and] focusing our eyes on Jesus, who is the Author and Perfecter of faith [the first incentive for our belief and the One who brings our faith to maturity], who for the joy [of accomplishing the goal] set before Him endured the cross, disregarding the shame, and sat down at the right hand of the throne of God [revealing His deity, His authority, and the completion of His work]." - Hebrews 12:1-2 (AMP)

....

I wrote a song called "To Notice You", which in this season is the deepest prayer of my heart and my favorite song. What we notice, look at and focus on matters so much. It affects our perspective and influences our decisions in our relationship with God, ourselves and others. Much more, there is so much God has to reveal to us about our lives and the world and so much He has in store for us, way more than we or anyone else has ever thought of or could ever imagine. If no eye has seen it or ear has heard it, wouldn't it make sense to spend time with the Originator of all these good and great plans thru prayer and His inspired written Word? Even as I write this, I am encouraged to lean in and recommit to keeping my desire to notice Jesus, as my priority. Today, meditate on the above verses and use your own words to talk to God in prayer in any way that seems fitting. Let Jesus meet you right where you are.

The pure in heart shall see God. Help me Lord to have a pure heart. I want to see you. God has prepared many things for me to see, hear. That my eyes have not seen or ears have not heard. God has prepared for me what I have not comprehend. Let my eyes be clear full of light so I can perceive, focus spiritualy on God, and the Body full of light. (God's word) and not Bad and Dark (with out God's word)

Day 24 – Royalty

~

"You will be a crown of splendor in the Lord's hand, a royal diadem in the hand of your God. No longer will they call you Deserted, or name your land Desolate. But you will be called Hephzibah, and your land Beulah for the Lord will take delight in you, and your land will be married. As a young man marries a young woman, so will your Builder marry you; as a bridegroom rejoices over his bride, so will your God rejoice over you." - Isaiah 62:3-5 (NIV)

....

The above passage is a passage that I have been meditating on for the past several years. I first held onto it when I participated in a Bible Study series on the Love of God. During the study, there were many verses shared with me but I chose to take one of the many and hold on to it for dear life. Since then, and more recently over a period of 2 years, I have been aiming to speak this specific passage verbally over my life - Breakfast, Lunch and Dinner - as if it was a meal in itself for me to digest. Within this time frame, I went to another ministry event, and during prayer, someone spoke key words from this verse over my life, which I took it in as a confirmation to God's promise that I was holding on to. This promise means everything to me. In Scripture, the promise was first spoken to an imperfect people. However, God's promise makes all the difference. 2 Corinthians 1:20 says, "For all of God's promises have been fulfilled in Christ with a resounding "Yes!" And through Christ, our "Amen" (which means "Yes") ascends to God for his glory." (NLT)

For this reason, you too in your journey with Christ can begin to hold onto His precious promises. For this day, the promise of Royalty - the promise of wholeness, belonging and taking up your purpose of reigning with Christ - is awaiting you if you believe. Let's pray:

Dear Jesus, I want to walk in your promise of Royalty and every other promise you have made for your people. Show me how and help me believe...

_____

_____

_____

_____

_____

_____

_____

_____

_____

_____

_____

_____

_____

_____

_____

_____

_____

_____

_____

_____

_____

_____

_____

Day 25 – Remain In Your Love

~

"I've loved you the way my Father has loved me. Make yourselves at home in my love. If you keep my commands, you'll remain intimately at home in my love. That's what I've done— kept my Father's commands and made myself at home in his love." - John 15:9-10 (The Message)

"...God is love." - 1 John 4:8b (NIV)

....

The first Scripture above is the words of Christ Jesus Himself.

His desire for us is to make ourselves at home in love; His Love. When I read this sentence I think of an actual home that you get to reside in and rest in; a safe place; a set-apart place. I don't know about you but I want to remain in love. I think everyone in this world would say the same. It is one thing to experience the love of God in Christ, but here Jesus says that He wants His followers to remain there. **Remain** in Love. Jesus gives us a very direct means to do so: Keep His commands.

The word "command" can cause a knee-jerk reaction for many. These days being commanded to do anything is not popular, sometimes for good reasons. But here, Jesus says keeping His commands is a direct tie to how intimately you experience love, real love. TV says that experiencing love has more to do with how fine your significant other is and how much they do for you; your marital status; how much money you have; how good you feel; how people treat you and how beautiful you are. However, that is not God's opinion or standard of remaining in love.

In addition, when you keep something, you hold on to it; you steward it. It is special to you. That is what we should do with God's thoughts that He has shown to us in His written Word. We may not understand it all, but when we approach it prayerfully and openly, God's thoughts slowly renews our mind.

Reading Scripture can seem like a duty to some at times. For others it can be a means to make themselves feel puffed up and full of knowledge; a means to check off lists of rules kept; or perhaps a way to justify their actions if they choose verses that already fit with how they are living, or their past experiences.

However, for those of us who truly want God in our lives and care about His opinion, growing in understanding, loving, trusting and obeying Scripture, is the place where we <u>remain</u> in Love.

Dear Jesus, teach me how to best keep Your commandments. I want to remain in love...

Remain - Walk - act - show love!
Gods love, for God is love. Keep
the Command of love. Be a doer
and not a hearer alone. But love
(do).

Day 26 – Trust and Breathe

~

"Do not be anxious about anything, but in every situation, by prayer and petition, with thanksgiving, present your requests to God. And the peace of God, which transcends all understanding, will guard your hearts and your minds in Christ Jesus." (Philippians 4:6-7 - NIV)

....

What do you fear? Let's take some time to give our fears to the Lord now. If there is no one you can trust, you can trust Jesus. He already knows not only your future but also the deepest part of your heart. Your fears could be about other people, they could be about yourself, your future, your past or what is happening in your life presently. Your fears could even be about what you think about God and what the response would be if you were honest about it. Regardless, Jesus already knows.

Dear Jesus ...

Jesus already knows. I Can Trust
Jesus. Help me not to fear anything.
Fear that is not from You.
I will pray about every thing and bring
all cares to you.

Day 27 –Happy

~

"To the person who pleases him, God gives wisdom, knowledge and happiness, but to the sinner he gives the task of gathering and storing up wealth to hand it over to the one who pleases God. This too is meaningless, a chasing after the wind." - Ecclesiastes 2:26 (NIV)

"His master replied, 'Well done, good and faithful servant! You have been faithful with a few things; I will put you in charge of many things. Come and share your master's happiness!' - Matthew 25:21 (NIV)

"But may the righteous be glad and rejoice before God; may they be happy and joyful." - Psalms 68:3 (NIV)

....

Happiness.

I think it gets a bad rap. Sometimes for good reasons but other times, it is treated as if the desire for happiness is a sin. Happiness is a God gift. It originated from Him and ultimately is given by Him.

There are many songs called "Happy". I decided to write my own version. Happiness gets a bad rap because many want others to understand that there will be hard times in life and you can't solely measure good feelings for the best choices. Many make decisions based on what feels good or what looks good versus what **is** good. There will be seasons of mourning, which is Biblical. There will be seasons of being on the battlefield even when you are doing the right thing. Even our Lord Jesus faced those seasons. Though Happiness is not an exact synonym for joy, happiness too is a gift from God and a fruit and reward of faithfulness to God. Therefore, it is fully acceptable to ask God for the gift of happiness and expect that it is part of His will for your life.

Dear Lord Jesus, help me understand what true happiness from You is and please give it to me according to your promise...

Happyness is a Gift from God,
a reward ③ for Faithfulness ④ (Fruite)
Happyness is part of Gods will for my
life.

Day 28 – Thank You

~

"In every thing give thanks: for this is the will of God in Christ Jesus concerning you." – 1 Thessalonians 5:18

"Still, You are holy; You make Your home on the praises of Israel" – Psalms 22:3 (The VOICE)

"Enter his gates with thanksgiving and his courts with praise; give thanks to him and praise his name." – Psalms 100:4 (NIV)

....

Day 28 Ends with a topic that is where you and I are to begin, going forward in our walk with Christ: <u>Thanksgiving</u>. It is so important to be thankful as we first approach God in prayer, but also throughout the day. He deserves our thanks and so much more. I know in this journey with Christ it may seem hard to figure out if we are tracking at times with where we are supposed to be. Nevertheless, one thing that we can do intentionally, and will help us stay close, is giving thanks. Here are various ways you can offer up your thanks to God:

- Write it down (keep a thanksgiving journal)
- Weekly offer up your words of thanksgiving in the company of Christ Believers;
- Every morning, wake up and give thanks ; End your day with Thanks - Begin to build your muscle of being a person of thanksgiving and praise;
- Weekly pick a friend or two that you can share intentionally what God has done for you, been to you, done through you, or given to you - that you are grateful for;
- Offer your thanks to God in your giving, (financially at your local church; with your talents and gifts and/time)
- Sing songs throughout the week (in your car, in your personal quiet time, at home, and if you are musically gifted - in the company of others at special events)

- Foster an atmosphere of Thanksgiving and Praise - Post your thanks on social media (that which you feel comfortable and is appropriate to share); Fill your space/s with songs and words of thanksgiving and praise.

Either way, make a commitment to acknowledging every good gift God has given you even during times that feel challenging. I challenge you to not leave one gift from God unacknowledged. The Lord Himself dwells, and makes His home, in your praise.

Dear Jesus, thank you for this time walking with you. Thank you also for the following gifts and blessings; I am so grateful for...

Give God Thanks every day and always. God deserves your Thanks and so much more. God dwells, lives in our praise and Thanksgiving. In every thing give thanks.

28 Days Completed!!!

Woohoo!

Next steps:

- Feel free to go through this devotional again and again. Each season in our walk with Christ is different even if we meditate on the same passages. Also, reminders are always needed.
- If this has been a blessing to you:
    - Share a copy of the book with a friend! Then,
    - Send me a note on my Facebook page (www.facebook.com/awilshiremusic) or on my website contact page at www.awilshiremusic.com
- No matter what, continue to walk with Jesus!

May God Bless You!!!

~ Angelica

psyche

<u>Soul</u>: Will - mind - Emotions
Reasoning Conciousness Feelings

Is a Living Being Creature that breathes.
Part of a person thats not phisical.
<u>apostle paul</u>: prayed: Our Body - Spirit and soul be made
blamless and keep.